THE COACHING POCKETBOOK

D0595184

By Ian Fleming & Allan J. D. Taylor

Drawings by Phil Hailstone

"Encapsulated my belief in the potential of people, and showed me how to translate this into appropriate action."
Jenny Hill, Training & Recruitment Manager, Gallaher Ltd.

"For UK plc to win a global marketplace it is essential for managers and leaders to understand learning and to develop coaching skills. This pocketbook provides a very readable insight into understanding the challenge."
Colin Ions, Consultant, HR Network.

"An amazing amount of ground has been covered in this little book – it unravels a complex subject in a very practical and easy to understand format."
Sarah Armstrong, Customer Services Manager, Eagle Star.

Published by:
Management Pocketbooks Ltd
Laurel House, Station Approach, Alresford, Hants SO24 9JH, U.K.
Tel: +44 (0)1962 735573   Fax: +44 (0)1962 733637
E-mail: sales@pocketbook.co.uk
Website: www.pocketbook.co.uk

First edition published 1998.
Second edition published 2003. 8th printing 2010.

© Ian Fleming & Allan J.D. Taylor 1998, 2003.

ISBN 978 1 903776 19 3

British Library Cataloguing-in-Publication Data – A catalogue record for this book
is available from the British Library.

Design, typesetting and graphics by **efex ltd**   Printed in U.K.

CONTENTS

CAUTION

Please don't read this book if:

- You don't enjoy working with people
- You haven't got the time to spend with them
- You don't believe that you can make an impact on their performance

as coaching could seriously change the way you operate at work!

If you've not done it before, coaching can take you out of your comfort zone; especially if you're used to controlling people and telling them what to do. You'll have to do some things differently.

WHAT IS COACHING?

WHAT IS COACHING?

A QUESTION

What do the world's top tennis players, golfers and athletes all have in common?

Apart from being very successful, and extremely rich, they each have a coach.
But why? The coach is there to help them:

- Build on their successes
- Work on the details that will sharpen up their skills, and improve their techniques
- Plan tactics ahead of important events
- Stay at the top in a very competitive world

Teams also can have coaches, where specialist individuals help certain groups or players. Coaches are also common in drama, speech, music; helping people through change as well as developing careers.

Excellence is never an accident

WHAT IS COACHING?

DEFINITION

The dictionary definition of a coach includes:
- 'a means of transport - a large motor vehicle which carries passengers from one point to another'
- 'someone who trains in a particular sport, gives people special teaching in order to prepare them for, say, an exam'

WHAT IS COACHING?

BUSINESS DEFINITION

In a business context coaching means **improving performance** at work, by turning **things people do** into learning situations, in a **planned** way, under **guidance**.

The key words are:

Improving performance	- using a range of learning experiences to bring about improvements
Things people do	- which become opportunities from which all parties can learn
Planned	- so as to get the most out of the situation
Guidance	- where the coach transfers knowledge, skills and experience

In short, it's about:

- Helping someone perform a skill or solve a problem better than they would otherwise have been able to
- Bringing about improvements at work; especially where a change in performance is required

WHAT IS COACHING?

A COACH'S ROLE

You may have built up the image from sport of a cap-wearing, gum-chewing, harassed-looking coach who typically suffers from the sidelines. Is this what it's all about?

Not really! However, the sports coach:

- Concentrates on improving performance
- Is committed to the players
- Talks of 'we' and 'us', not 'you' and 'them'
- Imposes no limits to the performance of individuals and teams
- Acts as a role model for others to follow
- Patiently works with individuals on the details of their performance
- Stands back and lets others take the credit
- Continuously learns from situations and people

These are the same things that managers do when coaching their staff.

A COACH'S ROLE

A coach helps people to perform better than they are currently doing, and develops their skills and confidence **over a period of time**. Results rarely happen overnight.

A coach thinks and operates in a way that:

- Lets go rather than wants to be in control
- Shares knowledge rather than keeps it private
- Adopts an open style with others by being available
- Involves people rather than keeps them at a distance
- Encourages others to go beyond their current levels of abilities
- Is a partnership

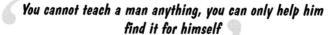

You cannot teach a man anything, you can only help him find it for himself

WHAT IS COACHING?

A COACH'S ROLE

A coach:

- Builds up a special relationship where people are treated as equals
- Learns from failure, or what went wrong, as well as success
- Gets results by doing rather than simply talking
- Empowers others - by sharing skills and experiences as well as values
- Plans an on-going relationship rather than a one-off event

Coaching is the key to creating a more open organisation, one that values people - their skills, ideas and contribution - and genuinely seeks to empower individuals. To be effective coaching must happen at every level in the organisation.

WHAT IS COACHING?

WHY COACHES ARE NECESSARY

- The pace of change requires managers to produce results quicker than before
- Traditional ways of achieving this, eg: keeping control of everything and passing out instructions, no longer work in today's world
- People want more from their work
  - it's the responsibility of managers to ensure that work, therefore, becomes more rewarding and fulfilling
- Today's managers have to manage the paradox of time
  - to create more time they will have to invest more time in their people; there is no other way
- To invest in people effectively, the manager
  - must have a fundamental belief that people can achieve whatever they believe is achievable **(The first rule of coaching)**
  - needs to continually raise that level of belief **(The second rule of coaching)**

WHO TO COACH

A whole variety of people at work are suitable candidates for coaching.

New Starters
Use coaching to complement a range of techniques, such as instructing, courses and working alongside others, to give people the basic skills to do the job.

Current employees
Look at those, individuals or teams, who you want to encourage to improve their existing performance, do more or realise their potential.

People you want to develop
Suitable courses aren't always available, or necessary; it's often far easier to coach.

Don't forget that you can also coach people more senior than you.

BENEFITS

FOR THE INDIVIDUAL

As an individual being coached, you:

- Gain from those you know and trust
- Learn at your own pace and from a one-to-one relationship
- Have an input over what and how you learn
- Develop the skills needed for your present as well as future jobs
- Can use the experience of those who have done it before and have learnt from their mistakes
- Will not be shown up and embarrassed if you make a blunder
- Can transfer the learning to situations you are facing
- Never stop learning and developing

 Learning is a treasure that follows its owner everywhere

WHAT IS COACHING?

BENEFITS
FOR TEAM AND COACH

A team benefits by:
- Becoming clear about the goals it has to achieve
- Focusing people in the right direction
- Raising the skill levels of the team members

The coach gains:
- By developing closer relationships
- Through discovering new ways of helping people
- From the feedback received
- By seeing people grow

WHAT IS COACHING?

BENEFITS

FOR THE ORGANISATION

The organisation gains by:

- Bringing individuals closer together and sharing knowledge, skills and experiences, so that all parties learn
- Making the most of work-related opportunities to learn from **real** situations
- Saving time spent away from work whilst attending courses or workshops
- Aiding the transfer of learning to the work situation
- Providing cost-effective ways of developing people
- Promoting a climate of continuous learning, support and ownership
- Improving the quality of work

Improve people and their productivity and you will improve your bottom line.

SUITABLE OCCASIONS

You may have formed the impression that you can only coach at certain times, eg:
- through setting objectives
- when delegating
- by working with new staff, etc.

Whilst these are correct, coaching is not only restricted to managers or to work situations. Anyone can coach, eg:
- formally, such as at an appraisal
- informally, on an ad hoc basis
- with colleagues, your boss, team members, peers, people in other parts of the organisation, outside it and even within your own family
- with individuals or groups of people.

You can coach people by passing on your knowledge and skills, as well as by helping them to realise their potential, and improve their skills.

It's not about how long you spend with people but how well you spend that time.

SUITABLE OCCASIONS

You have an opportunity to coach whenever:

- you are asked how to do something
- your advice is sought by others
- one of your staff says that they cannot do a particular job
- your opinion is asked for or a decision required
- you see a job or task that could be done quicker, better or cheaper
- mistakes are made.

In fact, any situation where you want people to raise their current levels of skills, abilities and overall performance.

Coaching always involves guidance and feedback; focuses on **how** to perform a skill or solve a problem; and can be planned but more often is ad hoc and 'on the spot'.

UNSUITABLE OCCASIONS

Coaching is not suitable:

- In an emergency that calls for action (but ensure you talk about it afterwards and the lessons learnt)
- If people don't really want to be coached
- When change is being forced through an organisation
- In formal disciplinary situations

WHAT IS COACHING?

WILL IT ALWAYS WORK?

No! Especially:

- In an **environment** where people are told what to do, given little freedom of choice and punished for their mistakes
- In an **atmosphere** that relies upon fear
- If the **relationship** between the coach and the other person(s) is not good (by itself coaching will not make a poor relationship better)
- When people are **forced** to learn; as coaching is a two-way process
- If people don't **believe** in it (should your natural style and preference be to tell, then coaching, and the spirit behind it, will sit uncomfortably with you)
- If you have **too many people** to manage or supervise
- Where people are working on **different agendas, goals or disagree about what has to be achieved**

LEVEL OF EXPERTISE

You don't have to be an expert. It helps your credibility, though, to know what you're talking about.

Being a good performer doesn't necessarily make you a good coach; top sports men and women don't always make successful coaches.

What you need above all else is the ability to encourage others to go beyond their current level of performance.

To do this you must:
- want to **share** what you know and your experiences with others
- be willing to **invest** time for the sake of others, and the organisation
- **believe** that people are capable of higher performance
- **not expect to take credit** for improvements in others
- **enjoy** working with people.

WHAT IS COACHING?

NECESSARY SKILLS

As a coach you need to be able to:

- Demonstrate excellent inter-personal skills in the areas of:
  - building rapport
  - asking questions/gaining information
  - giving and receiving feedback
  - listening
  - persuading, influencing and encouraging others
- Observe and correctly interpret what's happening; before, during and after
- Help others learn, and continue to learn yourself
- Think on your feet and tackle situations creatively
- Help others paint a picture of a higher level of performance

OTHER NECESSARY QUALITIES

Coaching is not only about having skills, but also about having:

- confidence in your own abilities and a knowledge of what you can't do
- a genuine affinity for people
- a belief in others and a real wish to see them succeed
- an ability to take second place and not seek any glory
- empathy, to see things from others' points of view
- sensitivity, especially knowing when to step in and when to be quiet
- patience and a willingness to make time for people
- a sense of humour

IS COACHING FOR EVERYONE?

Having said that we all have the potential to coach, it might not be for everyone.

Some people are just not suited to it. They may not see it as their job, lack the basic skills or the desire to help others, they may have excellent technical skills but be lousy with people.

Or, they may be under too much pressure to devote the time and energy required.

So, if you feel that it's not for you and that you can't coach, then ask someone who can. If you'd like to know more, and we hope that you will, then read on.

HELPING SKILLS

HELPING IN CONTEXT

VISION
Where does the organisation want to be?

VALUES & BELIEFS
What's important to both it and me?

CULTURE
How are things done around here?

JOB ROLE
What am I being asked/told to do?

COMPETENCY
What skills do I need to be good at?

ACTION
What plans do I have in place?

CHECKING
How will my progress be monitored?

HELPING
What resources are at hand to keep me on track and help me achieve?

TYPES OF HELPING SKILL

Coaching is but one way of helping individuals. What you choose depends on the:

- **Issue:** is it about performance or of a personal nature?
- **Style/method adopted:** whether you tell people what to do, or enable them to work it out themselves

(Source unknown)

DIFFERENCES

Advising	- giving opinions or information
Instructing	- teaching or informing others
Counselling	- encouraging someone to take responsibility for a problem or for improving a situation (often of a personal nature); in other words, to make decisions for themselves
Coaching	- a process by which the coach creates relationships with others that make it easier for them to learn; should coaching not work - for whatever reason - then the 'helper' may use counselling as a way of getting beneath the 'problem'
Mentoring	- helping people to realise their potential; it is usually carried out by someone outside your department and can combine elements of giving advice, counselling and coaching

COACHING AND INSTRUCTING

There are some subtle yet important differences between the two.

When instructing, you	When coaching, you	Suitable applications
control the rate of information	allow the learners to be more in control of the pace	helping someone put together a personal development plan
often tell people what to do	guide people, and together work out a solution or method	working with a team to develop new procedures, systems or methods
can be distant and impersonal	rely on the strength of the personal relationship	coaching somebody to deputise or stand in for you
can supply the same information to everyone	tailor your help and style to suit the needs of individuals and/or the group	encouraging a change in someone's performance
provide the knowledge on how to do things	encourage people to transfer what they learn to a variety of situations	using newly acquired time planning skills both at work and at home

COACHING AND INSTRUCTING

When instructing, you	When coaching, you	Suitable applications
often expect learners to be passive	actively involve those being coached in the process	if coaching someone to handle a difficult individual, you would get them to play out likely reactions to a variety of approaches
may put across one right approach or method to follow	encourage a range of alternative methods to try out	working out/helping plan possible negotiation strategies
try to avoid the learner making mistakes	use mistakes as an opportunity to learn	capturing the learning from a sales call that didn't go as planned
provide answers to questions	pose problems and discuss the learners' ideas	if you're offering to help someone who is introducing a change
often sit in judgement	encourage others to assess their own progress	a weekly review session with an individual who is new to the job

(Developed from the work of Sylvia Downs)

COACHING AND EMPOWERMENT

Empowerment may be familiar to you. Basically, it involves giving individuals responsibility and authority for making decisions at their own level. It allows those people doing the job to be more in control of what they do and how they do it.

It's based on the belief that problems are best solved by those people actually doing the job. In so doing, it challenges the traditional role of the manager being both the giver of orders and the resolver of problems.

Coaching can help the empowerment process by:

- Encouraging individuals to see opportunities to develop
- Creating an atmosphere where people want to learn
- Helping others to 'shout', ie: to ask for what they want

Coaching is the **skill** to complement empowerment.

COACHING AND EMPOWERMENT

'Empowerment within a framework' devised by Mark Brown of Innovation Centre, Europe, involves deciding upon the following areas:

'No go' - where the rules have to be obeyed, eg: confidentiality, safety, etc

'Yes, then go' - things that you can let go but people need to check with you first before tackling them

'Go, then inform' - areas that you are happy to let go, providing that people keep you informed

'Go' - where total empowerment is appropriate

Coaching can be used to move people from stage to stage. For example, at a 'no go' area tell people why they may not yet have the skills or experience, although with time they could. When they reach the 'go' areas you say, *'don't ignore me, from time to time tell me how you're getting on'*.

ASSUMPTIONS MADE

Underlying all these helping skills are certain assumptions:

- We all want to learn (certainly we all need to keep learning)

- Developing people is part of a manager's job (this is true and coaching is an effective way of making it happen)

- Anyone can coach (well, almost everyone)

- It's both good and relatively easy to form a close working relationship with people (it's not impossible but some need more work than others!)

- People want to be coached (but there are some who, on occasions, still prefer to be told)

HELPING SKILLS

POINTS TO REMEMBER

- Coaching is one of many ways of helping people

- There is a difference between **instructing**, which is essentially one-way, and **coaching**, where you enter a dialogue with others

- Empowering your staff is not simply letting them get on with their jobs; you have to be a good coach in order to make it work effectively

A STRUCTURE FOR COACHING

A STRUCTURE FOR COACHING

In simple practical terms, coaching involves four key stages:

C ompetency - assessing current level of performance

O utcomes - setting outcomes for learning

A ction - agreeing tactics and initiate action

CH ecking - giving feedback and make sense of what's been learnt

> There are numerous coaching models and structures, each with its own merits.
> Bear in mind though that they are for guidance only and should not be seen as
> some form of a straightjacket that will inhibit the coach's natural inclinations,
> intuition and knowledge of the individual.

A STRUCTURE FOR COACHING

 O A CH

COMPETENCY

When an opportunity to coach arises, eg: through a request for help or when someone makes mistakes, **avoid** the quick fix approach. The temptation is to jump in and take over, and tell people what to do. But don't.

The first stage of coaching is to find out what people are currently doing or have tried. In other words, what are they competent at doing? You need to do this in order to:

- Give you a base for starting to coach
- Influence what you do and the style you use

☞ What to do
Try asking: *'Show me what you've done'*
                'Tell me what you've tried'

Key skills are the ability to build rapport, and to get good quality information through skilful questioning, listening and observing.

A STRUCTURE FOR COACHING

C O A CH
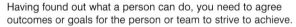

OUTCOMES

Having found out what a person can do, you need to agree
outcomes or goals for the person or team to strive to achieve.

**The secret for the coach is to create a compelling vision
for people to buy into.**

Outcomes are really objectives. However, all too often
objectives - though technically correct - fail to excite
and enthuse those on the receiving end.
The result is that they get lost somewhere in the
organisation's appraisals system.

When setting outcomes you also have an opportunity
to change people's perceptions of themselves.
For example, some people may have a view that
they just do a job. However, you may see them
as part of a team/organisation providing a
key service to others.

A STRUCTURE FOR COACHING

C A CH
OUTCOMES

The successful sports coach creates a picture, in the minds of those being coached, of what success will look like.

☞ What to do
As a coach in business you can do the same by asking the person:
- *'What do you really want to achieve?'*
- *'What will success look like, what will you see happening, hear yourself saying, feel?'*
- *'How worthwhile is that?'*
- *'How much does this inspire you?'*
- *'How far will it challenge and stretch you? (Is it worth putting energy into?)'*

It's important that their success doesn't depend on others and that it fits with the kind of person that they are or want to be.

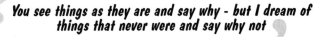

> **You see things as they are and say why - but I dream of things that never were and say why not**
>
> *- George Bernard Shaw*

(35)

A STRUCTURE FOR COACHING

C O A CH

ACTION

The action stage is where people have a go and actually do something.

To do this both parties have a part to play in:

- Looking for opportunities to try something
- Creating situations to practise and experiment
- Agreeing   - what can be done
  - what authority people will have
  - what freedom they have to make mistakes
    (for this reason be careful about activities
    with safety implications)

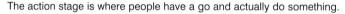

☞ What to do

Set up the action stage by asking questions and exploring options, eg:

- *'So what could we do/try?'*
- *'What opportunities have we got?'*
- *'How might we go about it?'*
- *'What if we tried...?'*

❝ *Behold the turtle... he makes progress only when he sticks his neck out* ❞
- James B Conant

A STRUCTURE FOR COACHING

C O A

CHECKING

As a coach you're trying to help the learner:
- Check progress against their outcome, ie: how they are doing
- Make sense of what they have learnt
- Improve through providing feedback
- Set higher outcomes if necessary; some skills are acquired slowly and in stages
- Have the confidence to do it themselves without needing your help

👉 What to do
You need to get them thinking; so ask plenty of open questions:
- *'How do you feel/how are you getting on?'*
- *'What appears to be working?'*
- *'Why do you think that is?'*
- *'What isn't working? I've noticed that you ...'* (Don't be afraid to tell people.)
- *'Why do you think that is?'*

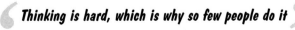 *Thinking is hard, which is why so few people do it*

A STRUCTURE FOR COACHING

CHECKING

If you are building up a skill in stages then you may need to go back and re-set the outcomes; possibly make them more demanding and raise the standards.

Look for opportunities for trying things out. You may need to adjust your style as people become more confident. You will also need to agree a different role for yourself as coach (ie: become more or less involved).

☞ What to do

Again, use lots of questions, eg:

- *'So where are we?'*
- *'What have we learnt so far?'*
- *'How do you feel about it?'*
- *'How might we apply this to ....?'*
- *'What about going on to/trying ...*(the next stage if appropriate)?'*
- *'How confident do you feel?'*
- *'What help might you still want?'*
- *'What are you going to do now?'*

COACHING SKILLS

RAPPORT

Coaching is built on the basis of creating and maintaining working relationships (you don't necessarily have to like people you coach, but it certainly helps).

The success of this will depend on the amount of rapport that exists between those involved. Without it there is likely to be suspicion; with it there's the basis for trust and co-operation.

Rapport means getting your behaviour in harmony with others. It assumes that people like people who are like themselves (it's very rare that you'll buy something from a person that you dislike). It is not simply about getting people to like you, but having the flexibility to behave in the same way as others.

BUILDING RAPPORT

People in rapport typically 'match' one another.

☞ **What to do**
When coaching, try:
- adopting the same posture and movements
- talking in the same tone and speed of voice
- mirroring the person's breathing rate
- using the same type of language

Don't make it too obvious, as rapport that works is an unconscious process. You may be doing it anyway without being aware of it, as it happens quite naturally.

BUILDING RAPPORT

Rapport is a powerful form of influencing and a key skill throughout all stages of the coaching sequence.

Building rapport is an intrinsic part of NLP (Neuro Linguistic Programming). NLP promotes the idea of matching and pacing (literally going at their speed) as a way of creating and maintaining rapport.

When you can match and pace you can lead, so don't expect others to come to you unless you first go to them.

☞ What to do
When building rapport with someone, it's essential that you:
- take care to avoid giving body signals showing disapproval of their actions
- try to put them at ease
- smile and use humour when appropriate
- share similar experiences
- work to gain their confidence
- use first names

COACHING SKILLS

QUESTIONING

When coaching you need information to help you find out where the person is coming from, what they have tried and what works.

Good information will increase your chances of providing appropriate help. However, you do need to be skilled at asking and using a range of questions.

☞ **What to do**
Use **open** questions to prompt a response and help you build a picture, eg:
- *'What have you tried?'*
- *'Why did you do it that way?'*
- *'What's worked .... what hasn't .... and why?'*
- *'What other ways ...?'*
- *'How could you ....?'*

COACHING SKILLS

QUESTIONING

TECHNIQUES

Blockbusting
When you are looking for more precise information, eg: *'what exactly have you tried?'*

Challenging
Questions to people who make generalisations, eg: 'it always happens' *'always?'*

Silence
Make time for your question to be answered. Allow silence to transfer responsibility for answering the question to the individual.

Testing understanding
When you want to establish whether or not an earlier contribution has been understood, eg: *'can we just check that we're talking about the same thing?'*

Summarising
Restating in a compact form what has gone before, eg: *'so what you're saying is that you've tried ....?'*

OBSERVATION

> *The real art of discovery consists not of finding new land but of seeing it with new eyes*

To be a skilled coach you may well have to change the way you look at both people and situations. We have a habit of:

- Putting individuals in boxes, ie: we form judgements about their abilities, potential and personalities

- Failing to spot situations where coaching may be appropriate, and failing to match people accordingly

Successful coaches open their eyes to all sorts of possibilities.

(45)

COACHING SKILLS

OBSERVATION

Observation is a key coaching skill. Many of us watch, but how many actually see what's happening? Observation is very powerful, especially when it brings to people's notice behaviour that is not normally commented upon. For example, if you were helping people improve their presentation skills you might notice and give feedback on their mannerisms.

As a coach you need to be able to:

- Spot what's happening and what's not
- Work out specifically what people are doing and how/why they do it
- Feed it back in a way that is constructive and helpful

👉 What to do
When observing:

- take in the overall picture; standing back may help, as will seeing it from different viewpoints; literally move around
- look out for sequences in which people do things, or for patterns of behaviour
- pay attention to any non-verbal signs/cues whilst you're talking to people or watching them carry out a job and, as a result...
- look to see if any patterns of behaviours emerge

LISTENING

If as a coach you want to come across as credible, gain people's respect, encourage them to have confidence in themselves, then you must **listen** and understand them.

Most people aren't trained to listen. We are all guilty of daily displaying our lack of skills when we:

- Hear only what we want to hear
- Fail to put ourselves in other people's shoes
- Think we know what people are talking about
- Listen to the words but miss the 'music', ie: emotions behind them
- 'Already listen', which means that we have made up our minds and only hear what we want to hear

All are disastrous mistakes if you want to succeed as a coach.

COACHING SKILLS

LISTENING

When coaching, you need to listen carefully to what people are telling you about what they have tried and discovered.

👉 **What to do**

You can show that you're doing this by:

- paying attention and showing an interest (don't only listen to the words but try to pick up the emotions behind them)
- reflecting back what you think they are saying (remember testing understanding and summarising)
- matching the behaviour of the speaker (rapport)
- avoiding distractions; don't look bored
- keeping your mouth shut and not talking!
- recognising it's not easy – most people tend to be 'hard of listening' rather than 'hard of hearing'

> *It is as though he listened and such listening as his enfolds us in a silence in which at last we begin to hear what we are meant to be*
>
> *- Lao Tse*

MATCHING PEOPLE'S WORLDS

Each of us represents and describes our world in a unique way. There are three main divisions:

Visually, in the form of pictures and images
(using words like *'I see'*, *'I get the picture'*, *'that's clear to me now'*)

Auditorially, through sounds and the spoken word
(*'rings a bell'*, *'strikes a chord'*, *'sounds good'*)

Kinaesthetically by physical or emotional feelings
(*'feels good'*, *'my gut reaction is'*, *'picked up what you meant'*)

Communications can break down for a variety of reasons. However, all too often we use our preferred way of representing the world, and wonder why there are problems!

See The Learner's Pocketbook for more information

MATCHING PEOPLE'S WORLDS

The skilled coach will spot the way people represent their world, critical when setting outcomes, and adjust the approach accordingly.

👉 What to do

To develop the skill next time you're having a conversation:

- listen to the words that people use
- see if a pattern emerges
- decide on their main preference (visual, sounds, feeling)
- now try to pick up on these signals and adjust your conversation accordingly

COACHING SKILLS

HELPING PEOPLE CHANGE

As a coach we often see potential or abilities in others that they don't see in themselves. Whilst a lot of our efforts are directed towards encouraging people to have a go, they might say **'I can't do that'**. This can prove to be a stumbling block to progress; where do you go from here?

Break down what they are saying and think of the implications.

➤ **'I'** is an **identity** or a label that they put on themselves. Typical comments could be:
- *'I've never been any good at that'*
- *'I always make mistakes'*

☞ **What to do**
Don't be afraid to challenge words like 'never' and 'always'

COACHING SKILLS

HELPING PEOPLE CHANGE

➤ **'can't'** is a **belief** that limits their ability to perform (beliefs strengthen and uphold values or what's important to people). What we value and what we believe determines why we do something.

Henry Ford said 'If you believe you can or can't do something, you're right'

☞ **What to do**
Ask questions, eg: *'how do you know that?'*

➤ **'do'** refers to **capabilities**, in other words how able are they to apply what they know and can do? Often this is influenced by how people see themselves (their identity) as well as what they value and believe.

☞ **What to do**
If people say *'that will never work here'* try replying *'but what would happen if it could?'*

COACHING SKILLS

HELPING PEOPLE CHANGE

➤ **'that'** is about **behaviour,** in other words what people say and do. Ideally, to encourage people to change, good role models are needed from whom to learn and grow in confidence. Sadly, all too often these are missing.

☞ What to do
The role of the coach is to encourage people to take on new behaviours. When faced with an objection try saying *'why not?'*

When coaching bear in mind that:

- All the levels influence each other; a shift in one affects what happens below it
- If you are trying to encourage people to change the way they think about themselves, this will often mean tackling the corresponding values, beliefs and behaviours

 Don't let what you can't do interfere with what you can do

LEARNING TO LEARN

If coaching is about 'turning the things people do into learning situations' how do you get all parties to learn?

Learning is about gaining knowledge or skill by study, experience, or being taught.

Learning to learn is about capturing the lessons from everyday experiences, good or bad. Learning the lessons from change, in particular, is a key skill for individuals, teams and organisations.

Helping others to learn and learning ourselves is not the same as teaching and being taught.

COACHING SKILLS

LEARNING TO LEARN

Help people develop their learning skills by:

- Consciously recognising and looking for everyday opportunities to learn,
  eg: within the job, by taking on more and working with others

- Raising its importance within the organisation, eg: include 'lessons learnt'
  into appraisal discussions and on the agenda of meetings

- Creating a climate which supports and encourages individuals to learn from each
  other and from things that actually happen (this will save you time, money and
  effort and stop you making the same mistakes)

- Bearing in mind that you're not trying to be a teacher, but someone who creates a
  situation in which others can learn

COACHING SKILLS

LEARNING TO LEARN

A coach needs to understand that effective learning only happens if people are able to:

- Involve themselves in actual experiences
  (an **activist** learning style where people are prepared to have a go)
- Stand back, observe and consider what's happened
  (a style known as **reflector**)
- Create abstract concepts and generalisations as a result
  (**theorists** who try to understand why things are done in a particular way)
- Actively experiment and try out ideas
  (**pragmatists** who are interested in putting the learning into practice)

Often because we learn best in a certain way, we assume that this will also work for others. Similar to ways in which people represent their world, this is not always the case.

LEARNING TO LEARN

Few people develop all four styles equally well.
Furthermore, research has indicated that we
all have preferences for particular styles.

However, the role of the coach
is to help people through
each stage of learning:

Activist

Pragmatist ⟷ **COACH** ⟷ Reflector

Theorist

Given our natural preferences,
the challenge is to get the:

activists - to stand back and make sense of what they have learnt
reflectors - to have a go and not simply watch others or engage in discussion
theorists - to try things out before being given the chance to ask questions
pragmatists - to experiment with how to do things prior to being taught techniques
or short cuts

LEARNING TO LEARN

Learning
is finding out what you already know

Doing
is demonstrating that you know it

Teaching
is reminding others that they know just as well as you

**therefore ....
we're all learners, doers and teachers**

From: Illusions - the Adventures of a Reluctant Messiah by Richard Bach

PLANNING LEARNING

For people truly to learn, they need to experience all four stages of the learning cycle. This means that you have to find ways of **involving** people, building in time to encourage them to **reflect** on what they have learnt.

Follow this by providing any necessary **explanations and reasons.**
Finally, link what has been learnt to **practical work situations.**

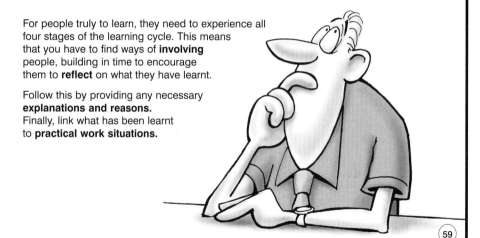

PLANNING LEARNING

Any element of learning will include facts to remember, concepts to understand, and skills to develop.

To help you coach, remember **MUD**

M emorise facts

U nderstand concepts

D o or practise skills

Help people develop the ability to:

- **M** emorise facts - by putting things in order, grouping them together, creating mnemonics

- **U** nderstand concepts - by explaining everything that can affect the issue, possible problems and how to get over them

- **D** emonstrate skills - by breaking them down into parts, building them up with practice, going at the learner's pace and not your own

CHOOSING A STYLE

At the action stage you are trying to give people the confidence:
- to have a go
- to discover what works and what doesn't
- to make mistakes and learn from them

You have to adopt a style that is suitable both to the situation and the person concerned.

Coach's involvement
Learner development

Use a **telling style** for those with low knowledge/skill

Help and guide those with basic abilities

Challenge and guide capable performers

Encourage the highly skilled to set new goals

A good coach moves up and down the continuum as appropriate.

COACHING SKILLS

DEVELOPING TRUST

Coaching involves an element of risk; sometimes things work, sometimes they don't.

In a coaching relationship, those being coached have to trust that the ideas, suggestions and experiences offered are helpful. The coach, in return, assumes that people will carry out what was agreed.

Trust is the basis of any coaching activity. As a coach you are trusted if:
- people understand why you are doing things
- you are true to your word and honest with yourself and others
- you have people's best interests at heart
- you know what you are doing
- your methods work and you're successful
- you trust people to be wrong

In the action stage trust is particularly important, especially when learning new skills or going outside one's comfort zones.

COACHING SKILLS

DEVELOPING TRUST

Ways to develop trust:

- Be yourself and share your experiences
- Show that you are open to ideas from those around you and prepared to give them a try
- Don't pre-judge people or situations
- Tell people how you feel
- Keep to your word; if you say you're going to do something, then do it
- Share relevant information when it's needed

GIVING FEEDBACK

Feedback is making people aware of what they are doing and the effect that it's having.

It's a valuable way of learning, especially in a coaching situation where you're trying to increase the learner's chances of success.

Remember that you can give feedback on what's working and what is not. The main point is to make it relevant and useful.

👉 What to do
When giving feedback:
- focus on behaviour that you have observed, *'I saw you doing...'*
- describe what you see happening, *'I notice that ....'*, but don't sit in judgement
- share ideas, *'what if you tried ....?'*
- explore alternatives, *'how could you ... what other ways ...etc'*

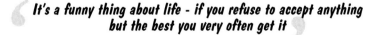

It's a funny thing about life - if you refuse to accept anything but the best you very often get it

COACHING SKILLS

GIVING FEEDBACK

If you fail to give useful feedback an important component of learning is lost.

Some simple frameworks that you can use when coaching include:

- Saying *'well done .....'* (give examples) before adding *'next time try .....'* (offering suggestions for improvement)
- Ideas for them to do *'more of ..... and less of .....'*
- Three things you have observed the person doing well and one suggestion

Remember
- Giving feedback is about providing plenty of reassurance and appropriate praise
- Take care not to demotivate people or revert to simply telling them how to do things
- Put yourself in their shoes and try to appreciate what they might be feeling and the difficulties they may be having
- Once they are armed with the feedback, you may very well want them to have another go

COACHING SKILLS

WARNING

Coaching is now an unregulated business, in which anyone can set up as a coach. So how do you spot the competent ones from the charlatans? Beware:

- The smooth talking/sales approach – good coaches don't push they pull
- The *'one size fits all'* method – the person who claims to have the answer for every situation. Good coaches use a range of approaches
- The person with limited experience – find out exactly what they've done
- People who make exaggerated claims about what they can do – they need to be challenged
- Coaches who want to work to their agenda and timescales – they've got it completely wrong
- People you simply don't like – trust your instincts and decline their offer
- Coaches who claim they can change your life

COACHING OPPORTUNITIES

APPLYING THE STRUCTURE

| **C** ompetency |
| **O** utcomes |
| **A** ction |
| **CH** ecking |

Yesterday's Actions

Today's Opportunities

Tomorrow's Plans

When coaching:
- Remember, it's never too late to coach on what happened yesterday
- Use what's happening today
- Think about what you want your people to be doing tomorrow

COACHING OPPORTUNITIES

APPLYING THE STRUCTURE

Before you start any coaching remember that:

- You need to approach it as someone who wants people to succeed, not as a boss, or a training and development specialist
- To be successful you have to demonstrate empathy, in other words get into other people's worlds (a common mistake is starting off from our own view and trying to get people to be more like ourselves)
- Coaching is about others, not about you (yet a lot of management training teaches us to think internally about ourselves, not externally about others)

When people's best work is done ... people say they did it themselves

- You need to plan what you are going to do; with experience it may come naturally but it can't initially be spontaneous, so read on for ways of making the most out of coaching situations

APPLYING THE STRUCTURE

It's never too late to talk about what happened yesterday by asking:
- *'what did you plan to do/what happened and why?*
- *'what did you learn, what might you do differently next time?'*

Look at what people are doing today as a coaching opportunity:
- *'talk me through what you are planning to do …'*
- *'what could go wrong … how would you handle it … can I make a suggestion?'*

Encourage people to talk through what they are intending to do tomorrow:
- *'what are you planning to do, how are you going to go about it?'*

YESTERDAY

Look for situations that have already happened, but don't leave it too long or else the moment will have passed.

Examples could be how individuals dealt with particular events, eg:

- Complaint from a customer
- Difficult member of staff
- Meeting that they ran
- An irate phone call
- A sales call/opportunity

COACHING OPPORTUNITIES

YESTERDAY

WHAT TO SAY

'Let's go back to what happened on ......'

Competency *'How did you think it went? Why was that?'*
Refer to specific events: *'What about...? What was your view of that?'*

Outcomes *'What were you trying to do, and why?'*

Action Referring to something that went badly: *'How could it have been prevented/what could you have done differently?'*
Picking up on something that went well: *'Why do you think that happened? What pleased you about it?'*
It's OK to point out to people what they might have done and why.

CHecking *'What did you learn/what were the lessons for the future? What might you do differently next time (to prevent the same things happening again)?'*
'How could you build on the good things that you did?'

Experience is a severe teacher: it tests first and gives the lessons afterwards

TODAY

What you're doing today provides numerous opportunities to share your experience and coach others, eg:

- How you organise your day
- Working through your mail
- Preparing for a meeting
- Tackling a problem or business topic
- Getting things done

COACHING OPPORTUNITIES

TODAY

You can also find coaching opportunities in your staff's work:

- If someone attends a course, talk to them and work out ways of applying the ideas gained, and skills learnt, back at work

- If someone is avoiding a difficult phone call or failing to confront poor performance, try running through their approach and what they might say and do

- If they are designing a new system, make sure that they are clear about what they have to achieve and explore possible options with them

- If they are putting together a proposal, help them to think through the advantages and consider how they would overcome any possible objections

COACHING OPPORTUNITIES

TODAY

WHAT TO SAY

'Let's have a look at ..... or tell me what are you doing today .....'

Competency   *'How capable/confident do you feel? Why/how come?'*

Outcomes   *'So what is it that you're trying to do/achieve, and why?'*

Action   *'How are you going to do it/show me what you are going to do.'*
          'Let's run through it together.'

CHecking   *'How useful was that (in giving you what you wanted)?'*
          'So, in conclusion, what are you going to do?'

As mentioned earlier a coaching model should not be seen as a restraint, something to inhibit your natural creativity and impulse. However, do not start or finish a coaching session without you and the other person being clear about: 1) *what they have tried;* 2) *What they want to achieve;* 3) *the actions they are going to take;* 4) *how they will measure (check) any progress*.

COACHING OPPORTUNITIES

TOMORROW

There are jobs that you might be doing regularly that others could do, with the right help and assistance. For example:

Activity	Preparation
Meeting visitors and showing them around	Involve them in the planning, background and arrangements
Being part of a working party or a committee	Look for situations which will broaden their thinking/exposure to others
Chairing certain meetings	Run through the agenda, and any potentially tricky areas
Preparing a budget	Use last year's as an example and build up in stages
Leading a project	They don't have to be an expert, you can help them with organisational and project management skills
Covering for holidays	Brief them about what's happening and any anticipated problems

COACHING OPPORTUNITIES

TOMORROW

In addition, opportunities may arise which, if they could be organised, provide chances to coach, eg:

- Job swapping - to gain experience and see things from another viewpoint
- Secondments - both within your organisation and outside
- Deputising and standing in for a boss or colleague
- 'Shadowing' a colleague - to see how they approach situations
- Preparing a training programme - to see what's involved
- Carrying out an appraisal - especially for the first time
- Keeping a learning log - as part of your job or your studies
- Being part of an interview panel - to share your judgements with others
- Organising an event - seeing things through from the original idea to the finished item

TOMORROW

WHAT TO SAY

'An opportunity has arisen which I think you could benefit from'

Competency   *'How do you feel about it? What reservations might you have and why?'*

Outcomes   *'This is what I have in mind. What are your thoughts and ideas?*
Let's work out what success might look like.'

Action   *'What could we do to make this happen? What if we did ....?'*

CHecking   *'So how do you feel about that?'*
'In conclusion what we've agreed then is to ....'

> ### *Man's mind once stretched by a new idea never regains its original dimension*
> - Oliver Wendell Holmes

COACHING TEAMS

Coaching a team presents a different challenge from simply coaching individuals. For a start, there are more people, each with their own level of skill and needs.

In sport, specialist coaches concentrate on certain positions; in business, the coach has to deal with the whole team.

Teams have the potential to motivate each other, set their own goals and coach or help themselves. Don't forget that team members need the same coaching skills as individuals, especially if you want them to influence others' behaviours.

If you can get them to start working for each other and sharing their own experiences in a constructive way for the good of the team, then you have made a breakthrough in teamworking.

With teams there are more factors to consider, yet the same rules apply, eg: asking where we are now, where we want to be, how we can get there, etc.

COACHING TEAMS

When you are coaching teams you are demonstrating leadership skills. The techniques that you use are the same as with individuals.

☞ What to do

To get the best out of your team as a coach try:

- setting aside time with them over and above any regular meetings to look at how you can work together

- deciding the agenda with them in advance and issues to address during these sessions

- agreeing team goals, ie collective targets that require collaboration – not imposing any limits on their potential performance: teams can do extraordinary things

- gaining regular feedback from them on your effectiveness as a coach – and use it

- being a model of the behaviours that you want to encourage in the team. Therefore, whatever you all agree is important for the team, eg respect, commitment or trust – make sure that you demonstrate these behaviours.

COACHING TEAMS

👉 What to do

As a coach:

- be consistent in your behaviour. Don't just put on your coaching hat when you have all the team together; you are a coach all of the time. In sport the manager is often the person who picks the team. The coach(es) develops the individual's skills and competencies to achieve over and above what's expected. In this role they are always coaching

- never focus on behaviours alone; always concentrate on the performance levels required and the behaviours associated with success

- remember that teams – in the true sense – have people who can 'play in more than one position' and help each other out when the need arises. As a coach, work to extend people's range of skills, capabilities and confidence

- don't make things too complicated or you run the risk of losing people's interest, energies and commitment. Simplicity enhances clarity of decision-making, pace and performance, and ultimately leads to better results

SELF DEVELOPMENT

Coaching is a great way to bring about other people's self development:

- When you are coaching you are more able to help individuals and together come up with a realistic plan

- Should you not be skilled as a coach, the help you can offer may be limited

Paradoxically, if you're a good coach, you could also be doing yourself out of a job by providing people with what they need, and helping them become more confident. Once people understand how they learn, any learning needs less structure and often less from you.

COACHING OPPORTUNITIES

COACHING UPWARDS

- Most managers will see coaching colleagues and staff as an acceptable activity but will have difficulty in doing the same with their boss

- There is often a mindset that the boss knows better, yet in today's fast changing world, with flatter structures and cross-functional working, this isn't always the case

- Individuals need to break the mindset and view their boss differently and as less of an expert than they may previously have thought

- To coach upwards, you need all the skills already described and, in particular:
  - know what it is that you want to achieve and why
  - use your knowledge of the individual and your personal judgement of how best to approach them
  - make sure that they have confidence in you as a credible person
  - choose your moment ... timing is important

COACHING OPPORTUNITIES

MEASURING THE OUTCOME

How do you go about measuring the success of your coaching efforts?

To do this you have to:

- be clear about what you want the coaching to achieve. This is where setting clear outcomes at the early stage of the coaching process is critical
- focus on what the coaching has achieved; in other words, look at the outcome or effect rather than the way that the coaching was carried out

Ask yourself what people have done differently as a result.

Finally, get the individual to self-assess, to talk through their own progress and measure themselves against what they set out to do.

POTENTIAL PITFALLS

TIME AND STYLE

You would like to coach but find that you have no time

If so … look for opportunities to coach, rather than periods of time. Remember that it's the quality of the help that you give, not the amount of time that is key.

Half-way through a session you realise that you're telling and not coaching

If so … stop talking and invite the other person to summarise; ask for a view, opinion or ideas; ask more open questions.

RESULTS

You don't get the results that you were hoping for from the coaching

If so … ask yourself why this was, look at your own style and jointly re-set the goals.

Still no improvement after weeks of coaching

If so ... (again) ask yourself why this might be. Is it to do with you or the other person? Is it really a coaching issue or something requiring counselling?

Coaching relationships become stale and bogged down

When this happens both parties have a problem. In our experience a coach should coach an individual for 12 to 18 months to ensure that each session remains 'fresh', unique and stimulating. Beyond this there is a danger of becoming stale. To negate this requires a completely fresh look at the desired outcome and the coaching relationship, and both parties challenging the reasons for continuing.

POTENTIAL PITFALLS

IMPASSE?

The person you are coaching believes there is nothing they can do to improve their situation

If so … ask challenging and blockbusting questions (page 44); keep quiet (silence is powerful).

No notice is taken of the feedback that you give

If so … get the other person to explain in their own words what it is that you are saying. It may be that they are not hearing the words or the messages.

RELATIONSHIPS

Relationships aren't good

If so … work on the relationship since coaching by itself will not make it (the relationship) better.

Coaching somebody who you have 'written off'' in your own mind

If so … avoid this mind-set, difficult though it might be. Where's your evidence? Everyone has potential; the skill of the coach is to discover what it is and explore it to the full.

(89)

POTENTIAL PITFALLS

HARPING BACK

Instead of focusing on the future you get bogged down in the past – in history

If so … make sure that the lessons from the past are clearly identified and show how they can be linked to the future. Should the past be mentioned, remind people that you're talking about the future.

The person you are coaching is afraid to try new suggestions and ideas because of previous experiences

If so … encourage them to agree a trial period; coach them through some 'what if' situations so they have ideas on how to deal with potential problems.

POTENTIAL PITFALLS

'NOT FOR ME!'

The person you are coaching thinks they are better than they really are

If so … ask for examples to support their view of themselves; give personal feedback, followed by silence!

Person has no interest in being coached

If so … ask yourself why this might be (their behaviour could hide a variety of reasons); try various approaches and if you still get the same reaction, give up.

CHANGE OF STYLE

Half-way through a coaching session, you find yourself pushing your own solution on the other person

If so … stop what you are doing straight away. Encourage the individual to think of his or her own ways of tackling the situation; try planting a seed of an idea to consider, along the lines of *'What if … ?'*.

You as a coach become complacent

This can happen for many reasons. It could be to do with your own ability. If this occurs then get someone to coach you.

Coaches who take their role seriously develop themselves. They know what it's like being coached and are conscious of the stages of learning that you pass through. Bear this in mind if you are looking for a coach: what are the implications for you if you choose a coach who is not being coached themselves?

CHECKLIST

CHECKLIST

PLANNING TO COACH

Questions to ask:

- 'What opportunities have I got in my current role to coach either my staff, peers or boss?'
- 'Why would coaching help me or the situation we're in, as opposed to simply telling people what to do or ignoring what's happening?'
- 'Which of my staff would coaching help?'
- 'What specific improvements do I want to see?'
- 'What level of performance is required or are people capable of?'
- 'What actions do I/we need to take?'
- 'What will success look like for us?'
- 'What are the important questions that I need to ask?'
- 'When will I have to be more directive and less questioning?'
- 'How and when would we check progress?'
- 'What might prevent us from succeeding and what would we do?'

The harder I work the luckier I become - Gary Player

CHECKLIST

A WORKED EXAMPLE

Taking the earlier example of someone reluctant to make a presentation to the directors, a way of tackling the situation would be as follows:

Planning
Decide for yourself:
- What it is that you want them to do and why
- What their reactions are likely to be and how you might cope with them
- What you might be thinking if you were in their shoes and, again, how you would deal with any concerns
- What the timescale is (eg: next week or next month)
- Whether or not you have the time available to help them do it well if you offer to coach
- What your initial approach to them will be

First meeting
- Set out your position carefully, explaining what you want them to do and why
- Invite feedback and test understanding to clarify what they are saying
- Get agreement that a problem or concern exists, don't avoid the issue
- Seek solutions by offering your ideas, inviting theirs, and jointly seeking compromise or the best solution

A WORKED EXAMPLE

Working through the **C O A CH** model, ask:

Competency
- *'Where are we starting from?'*
- *'What experience have you had in making presentations, to what sort of people?'*
- *'How did you find it went/what did you learn?'*
- *'How did you go about it?'*

Outcomes
- *'What I would like you to do ...'*
- *'How do you feel about that?'*
- *'What questions do you have?'*
- *'How do you see it?'*
- *'What do you need to know before you can start?'*
- *'Any ideas as to how you will put it together?'*
- *'What help do you want from me?'*
- *'Why don't you go away and start putting it together?'* (make sure you stay in touch in case they need you)

CHECKLIST

A WORKED EXAMPLE

Action

Set up a situation where you can watch them run through the content
- *'Let's run through what you're doing'*
- *'How have you approached it, what was
  the thinking behind this?'*

Challenge and influence their thinking
- *'Why are you planning to do it that way?'*
- *'What other ways could you tackle it?'*
- *'What if you .....?'*

CHECKLIST

A WORKED EXAMPLE

CHecking

Give them feedback, eg:
- *'That worked well ... how about/what if you ...?'*
- *'How comfortable do you feel about that?'*
  (don't impose your way of working, but make sure you influence standards)
- *'What further help do you want from me?'*

Face them with some potential situations:
- *'What if the meeting was running late and they only gave you 10 minutes, what's the main message that you want to get over?'*
- *'What's the most difficult question they could ask, how would you respond?'*

Review

Don't forget to have a follow up:
- *'How did that go?'*
- *'What went well (and why)? What didn't go as you expected (why)?'*
- *'How did you feel when you were doing it? How do you feel now? What did you learn from it?'*
- *'If you were doing it again what would you do differently?'*

CHECKLIST

PROFORMA

COACHING CHECKLIST	
Situation	
Initial Planning	
Competency	
Outcomes	
Action	
Checking	
Review	

Write your own words

QUESTIONS FOR INDIVIDUALS

Remember, those on the receiving end of coaching have a need to be:

- Treated fairly and not patronised
- Led at their pace, not yours
- Told what they do well, and made aware of mistakes made, and current level of performance
- Guided by a role model they can respect
- Encouraged to go further than their current level

The experience of being coached should be a positive one!

AND FINALLY

AND FINALLY

PUTTING IT INTO PRACTICE
THINK BEFORE YOU ACT

If you've read the book and would like to try coaching, remember the caution we gave at the start.

For you, it might mean adopting a new approach and evolving a change of style. If you start to question people, when in the past you've been telling them, they might wonder what on earth's going on!

So find somebody with whom to talk it through. Look around for some suitable training. In so doing practise your questioning skills and probe those who are running courses and workshops.

Remember that coaching is an unregulated industry. What you are looking for in a coach is someone you can trust to help you help yourself.

GETTING A PAYOFF

Most of us think about the **past**, talk about the **present**, and not much about the **future**.

Yet the future is where the payoff lies.

To obtain a better return from your investment in people, send fewer of them on courses, and put your efforts into **coaching** to develop them - at work - for **tomorrow**.

READING LIST

Developing High Performance People - the Art of Coaching, *Mink, Owen and Mink, Addison Wesley*

Everyone needs a mentor, *David Clutterbuck, Institute of Training & Development*

One-to-one training and coaching skills, *Buckley and Caple, Kogan Page*

Watch the 'Green Movie', *Melrose Video Productions, for details of the* 'Empowerment within a framework' *concept.*

You may find the following Pocketbooks particularly useful for situations in which you can coach:

The Trainer's Pocketbook
The Creative Manager's Pocketbook
The Interviewer's Pocketbook
The Time Management Pocketbook
The Appraisals Pocketbook
The Business Writing Pocketbook

The Negotiator's Pocketbook
The Meetings Pocketbook
The Mentoring Pocketbook
The Empowerment Pocketbook
The Telephone Skills Pocketbook
The Assertiveness Pocketbook

DEVELOPING PEOPLE
Pocketbook

A pocketful of ideas, tips
and techniques to help
managers identify staff
development needs and
bring about
successful learning

STAFF
TRAINING
NEEDS

MR. ROBINSON
MANAGER

Ian Fleming

Other titles by Ian Fleming in this series are:
People Manager's; **Teamworking**; **Time Management** & **Virtual Teams**.

THE MANAGEMENT POCKETBOOK SERIES

Pocketbooks (also available in e-book format)

360 Degree Feedback
Absence Management
Appraisals
Assertiveness
Balance Sheet
Business Planning
Business Writing
Call Centre Customer Care
Career Transition
Coaching
Communicator's
Competencies
Creative Manager's
C.R.M.
Cross-cultural Business
Customer Service
Decision-making
Delegation
Developing People
Discipline & Grievance
Diversity
Emotional Intelligence
Employment Law
Empowerment
Energy and Well-being
Facilitator's

Feedback
Flexible Workplace
Handling Complaints
Icebreakers
Impact & Presence
Improving Efficiency
Improving Profitability
Induction
Influencing
International Trade
Interviewer's
I.T. Trainer's
Key Account Manager's
Leadership
Learner's
Management Models
Manager's
Managing Assessment Centres
Managing Budgets
Managing Cashflow
Managing Change
Managing Customer Service
Managing Difficult Participants
Managing Recruitment
Managing Upwards
Managing Your Appraisal

Marketing
Meetings
Memory
Mentoring
Motivation
Negotiator's
Networking
NLP
Nurturing Innovation
Openers & Closers
People Manager's
Performance Management
Personal Success
Positive Mental Attitude
Presentations
Problem Behaviour
Problem Solving
Project Management
Psychometric Testing
Resolving Conflict
Reward
Sales Excellence
Salesperson's
Self-managed Development
Starting In Management
Strategy

Stress
Succeeding at Interviews
Tackling Difficult Conversations
Talent Management
Teambuilding Activities
Teamworking
Telephone Skills
Telesales
Thinker's
Time Management
Trainer Standards
Trainer's
Training Evaluation
Training Needs Analysis
Virtual Teams
Vocal Skills
Working Relationships
Workplace Politics

Pocketfiles

Trainer's Blue Pocketfile of Ready-to-use Activities

Trainer's Green Pocketfile of Ready-to-use Activities

Trainer's Red Pocketfile of Ready-to-use Activities

19.05.10

About the Authors

Ian Fleming MA DMS Dip Ed, works as a coach with individuals and
teams helping them achieve results by raising their level of performance
and confidence.

Should you want to talk to Ian about his ideas and approach,
contact him at:
'Summer Bank', 38 Abbey Road, Llandudno, North Wales LL30 2EE.
Tel. 01492 877539   e-mail: ian@creativelearning.uk.com

Allan J.D. Taylor has over 20 years' experience as a training and
development manager, mainly in the brewing industry. His interest in
coaching resulted from realising that most of what he did as a trainer
didn't work.

Coaching is becoming an increasingly important skill for managers and
those interested in improving performance and developing individuals.
Practical experience has led the authors to believe that, done well,
coaching can raise performance levels beyond the accepted norm.

However, the current emphasis on winning and achieving targets - rather
than raising performance levels - is, perhaps, the wrong focus. If you want
people to reach what they think is their potential, and go beyond it, you
don't need to impose a ceiling.

ORDER FORM

Your details

Name _____

Position _____

Company _____

Address _____

_____

_____

Telephone _____

Fax _____

E-mail _____

VAT No. (EC companies) _____

Your Order Ref _____

Please send me:

		No. copies
The Coaching	Pocketbook	
The _____	Pocketbook	
The _____	Pocketbook	
The _____	Pocketbook	

Order by Post
MANAGEMENT POCKETBOOKS LTD
LAUREL HOUSE, STATION APPROACH,
ALRESFORD, HAMPSHIRE SO24 9JH UK
Order by Phone, Fax or Internet
Telephone: +44 (0)1962 735573
Facsimile: +44 (0)1962 733637
E-mail: sales@pocketbook.co.uk
Web: www.pocketbook.co.uk

Customers in USA should contact:
Management Pocketbooks
2427 Bond Street, University Park, IL 60466
Telephone: 866 620 6944   Facsimile: 708 534 7803
E-mail: mp.orders@ware-pak.com
Web: www.managementpocketbooks.com